VAUX HALL BRANK
FREE PUBLIC LIBRARY

D0944464

LATINOS IN THE LIMELIGHT

VAUX HALL BRANCH
FREE PUBLIC LIBRARY

Christina Aguilera

Antonio Banderas

Jeff Bezos

Oscar De La Hoya

Cameron Diaz

Jennifer Lopez

Ricky Martin

Selena

CHELSEA HOUSE PUBLISHERS

LATINOS
IN THE
LIMELIGHT

Oscar De La Hoya

VAUX HALL BRANCH
FREE PUBLIC LIBRARY

Rob Quinn

CHELSEA HOUSE PUBLISHERS
Philadelphia

Frontis: *With his talents and skills in the ring, Oscar De La Hoya has won titles and fame as well as the nickname Golden Boy.*

Produced by
21st Century Publishing and Communications, Inc.
New York, New York
http://www.21cpc.com

CHELSEA HOUSE PUBLISHERS

Editor in Chief: Sally Cheney
Production Manager: Pamela Loos
Art Director: Sara Davis
Director of Photography: Judy L. Hasday
Managing Editor: James D. Gallagher
Senior Production Editor: J. Christopher Higgins
Publishing Coordinator: James McAvoy
Project Editor: Anne Hill

© 2001 by Chelsea House Publishers, a subsidiary of Haights Cross Communications. All rights reserved. Printed and bound in the United States of America.

The Chelsea House World Wide Web address is
http://www.chelseahouse.com

First Printing

1 3 5 7 9 8 6 4 2

Library of Congress Cataloging-in-Publication Data

Quinn, Rob.
    Oscar De La Hoya / by Rob Quinn.
        p. cm. – (Latinos in the limelight)
    Includes bibliographical references and index.
    ISBN 0-7910-6098-5 (hardcover) — ISBN 0-7910-6099-3 (pbk.)
    1. De la Hoya, Oscar, 1973– —Juvenile literature 2. Boxers (Sports)—United States—Biography—Juvenile literature. [1. De la Hoya, Oscar, 1973– . 2. Boxers (Sports). 3. Mexican Americans—Biography.] I. Title. II. Series.

GV1132.D37 Q85 2000
796.83'092—dc21
[2]   00—059653
                                                                                             CIP
                                                                                             AC

J B
DE LA HOYA, O.

c. 1   6-01

$17.95

Dedication: *To Mom and Dad, for all I have learned, will learn, and missed learning from you.*

CONTENTS

FOR RESPECT

It is rare for a man to meet his childhood sports idol—let alone compete against him. But in September 1998 boxer Oscar De La Hoya had a chance to do just that, and for the second time. On this occasion he was determined not to leave any doubt as to the outcome.

Oscar's first meeting with Julio César Chávez had been in June 1996. The two had entered the ring for that first bout just before 9 P.M. in the outdoor arena at Caesars Palace in Las Vegas, Nevada. The temperature was still in the 90-degree range; under the ring lights, it was probably closer to 100. It was the 100th fight of César Chávez's career, and he had lost just once. Despite only fighting 22 professional bouts in his career, Oscar was undefeated, and he entered the ring favored to win.

As Oscar stepped through the ropes first that night, the two opponents' similar backgrounds could not have been far from his mind. He wore a bright red robe that bore the national colors of both the United States and Mexico. He knew Chávez would enter soon with his

---

Oscar (left) and Julio César Chávez strike fighting poses as they weigh in for their 1998 rematch. Although Chávez was the favorite, Oscar was determined to win this bout and gain the respect of Chávez, the boxer who had been his childhood idol.

traditional red headband and the colors of his native Mexico on his robe.

Oscar's father, Joel De La Hoya, had come to the United States as a young man. A close-knit extended family never let Oscar forget his roots in Mexico. Of course, if the pro-Chávez crowd of 16,000 that was watching the sold-out match and waving plenty of Mexican flags had been on Oscar's side, it would have been more than a reminder.

On top of everything else, Chávez owned the World Boxing Council (WBC) superlightweight title belt. With the exception of a three-month span, he had held the belt since 1989. The WBC is one of the three boxing organizations—along with the International Boxing Federation (IBF) and the World Boxing Association (WBA)—in which holding a title still brings respect. This truly was more than just another fight.

The bell finally rang. The fighters started cautiously. Most spectators thought they were just feeling each other out, as often happens when fighters first meet in the ring. Then after a brief exchange of punches midway through the opening round, blood began streaming down Chávez's face. He was cut.

The referee called the ring physician to look at the cut, but the fight continued. Oscar gained confidence as the round continued, and he kept Chávez from being effective by hitting the champion with lightning-quick combinations to the head. Oscar was moving in and out so quickly that the older and slower Chávez missed badly and often.

Then Chávez broke through to score near the end of round two. However, his temper flared in round three after Oscar appeared to shove him during an exchange. Chávez

landed the best blow of the fight early in round four, a hook that brought the crowd to its feet. He followed with a barrage of blows that sent Oscar reeling onto the ropes. The young boxer fought back with such fury that blood spewed from Chávez's face, and the fight was stopped.

"When I got hit, I didn't feel the punch," Chávez remarked after he had lost the fight. "I have lots of fight left in me. I want a rematch."

In their first match in 1996, Oscar (right) lands a punch that sends Chávez reeling. Oscar's hard-driving hooks and jabs were devastating, and finally gave the young fighter the win on a technical knockout.

He said he wanted two more fights and definitely "another shot at Oscar." An elated Oscar said he kept his composure and followed his battle plan during the match. "I knew if he got injured it would be a big problem for him. He's a true warrior but when I cut his eye and broke his nose with a left hook—I think I heard it break—I knew I had him."

Oscar was ahead on all of the scorecards when the match ended. One reporter wrote that the young fighter "showed the footwork of a dancer and quickness of a cat."

For millions of proud Mexicans, including many disbelieving spectators among the 16,000 at the sold-out bout, Chavez's defeat was like the fall of a treasured national monument. Oscar, whose ability to take a punch and whose desire to win fights had been questioned at times, had silenced some critics and propelled himself toward megastardom.

"Best finisher since Ray Leonard in his prime," an impressed Seth Abraham, president of HBO Sports, said of Oscar. "No one else is even close. He's simply a killer."

Dino Duva, who promoted WBC welterweight champion Pernell Whitaker at the time, also liked what he had seen of Oscar. "Chávez had nothing, but you have to give the kid credit," Duva said. "He saw the opening and he picked Chávez apart. He finished him off nice."

At age 23, Oscar had already won three world championships in three weight divisions in only 22 fights. He had also established his goal of winning six world crowns in a career that he says will be full, but brief. He had received nearly $9 million, becoming one of the few nonheavyweights in boxing history to

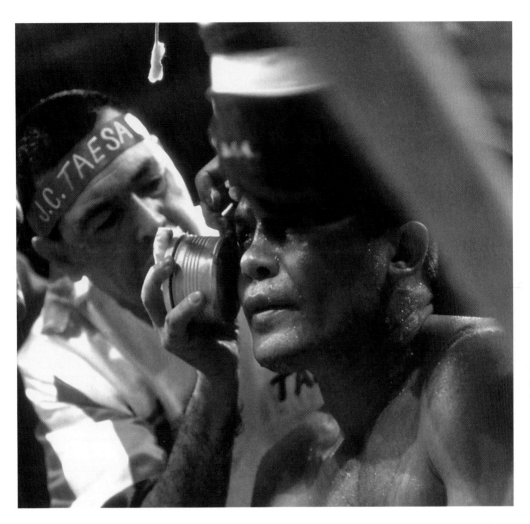

attract a multimillion dollar paycheck. For Oscar, however, something was still missing. He wanted a clear victory over Chávez—one that wasn't tainted by a cut.

The prefight buildup to the September 18, 1998, rematch had been surprising to some after such a one-sided fight the first time. Many predicted more of the same the second time around. But to Oscar, this fight was about more than winning. It was about respect.

"He's made up excuses after he lost to me

A bloodied Chávez has a cut attended to during his rematch with Oscar in 1998. Fighting fiercely to retain his welterweight title against the challenger, Oscar pummeled Chávez for eight rounds until Oscar was declared the winner on a technical knockout.

the first time," Oscar commented afterward. "If he was a real man he would admit he lost and he still refuses to do so."

Chávez insisted the outcome would have been different in the first fight had he not been cut. "How am I supposed to give him respect if I was cut?" Chávez asked. "It doesn't make sense. I didn't give him respect because he didn't earn it."

After a doctor declared Chávez's face was in fine condition to fight, Oscar was thrilled. "I'm very happy the doctor went to the podium and said he's not cut anymore," he said. "I want to knock him out, not stop him on cuts."

It wasn't long after Chávez finally climbed into the ring that Oscar was making his point with his fists. Chávez tried to get in closer to the taller champion, but Oscar's jabs began wearing him down.

By the middle rounds, there was little doubt of the outcome. Chávez made his presence known at times, rocking Oscar back with lefts and rights. But the jabs Chávez endured bloodied him over both eyes.

"I think he's getting tired now," Oscar told his trainer after the fifth round.

The crowd continued chanting "Chávez! Chávez!" as they had since the preliminary bouts. From the middle rounds on, the fighters went toe to toe. Late in the eighth, Oscar jolted his opponent with a left hook. He then moved in for the knockout, ending the round with a flurry.

Chávez followed Oscar to his corner when the bell sounded, claiming the blows were late. No foul was called, but the punches had caused their desired effect. Just seconds later, Chávez sat on his stool and the fight was halted because he could not continue. Oscar was victorious again.

About the only remaining question for the near-sellout crowd of 17,125, and an international pay-per-view audience of millions, was who had stopped the fight? Flip Homansky, the ringside physician, said it wasn't him. Richard Steele, the referee, said it wasn't him. So was it Chávez's corner, or was it Chávez himself as he sat bleeding on his stool after the eighth round?

"He quit on me," Oscar said in an interview after the fight during which he wore dark glasses to hide his swollen eyes.

Chávez bitterly proclaimed in Spanish, while blotting blood from a severely cut lower lip: "I am a man." He tapped his heart repeatedly. "Mano! Mano!"

Oscar was the winner in the eyes of most spectators. "I definitely think he [Chávez] quit," said Ike Quartey, the unbeaten World Boxing Association welterweight champion who was scheduled to face Oscar next. "He was tired, he couldn't go on." Either way, Chávez was beaten. He was behind on all three judges' cards, and he had been bleeding from the nose for several rounds. His crimson face showed glove burns, and blood oozed from cuts and the swollen lip.

Still, Chávez, the 6-1 underdog, had shown the courage that had carried him through 106 fights, 101 victories, and only three losses and two draws over 18 years. In the end, Oscar had already acknowledged Chávez's greatness after their first duel.

"This fight was very tough on me because Julio César Chávez is my idol," Oscar said. "He will always be my idol. He is a great champion, a great person. But my job is to win fights."

An elated Oscar celebrates his win over Chávez in 1998. It was a hard-fought battle for both boxers, and even though Oscar won on a technical knockout, he finally earned the respect of Chávez, who acknowledged that Oscar had beaten him.

When the media asked Oscar if he had sympathy for Chávez, he replied: "I had no feeling in that ring toward him. Once I step inside that ring, I become a different person. In the ring, Julio César Chávez was my enemy."

While Oscar did not get the devastating knockout he wanted in the second fight, he did get the respect of the fighter he once idolized. The two duelists hugged at the end, and Chávez saluted the champion as he left the ring.

"In the ring, Oscar and I said what we have talked about in the past is forgiven," Chávez acknowledged. "We shook hands like friends. He's a great fighter."

Even more important to Oscar than the fight was that he finally heard the words he wanted to hear. They came from the bloodied mouth of Julio César Chávez, who was finally ready to give Oscar his due.

"You beat me," Chávez whispered as the two embraced in the middle of the ring that Friday night in Las Vegas.

BORN IN EAST LOS ANGELES

During Christmas of 1976, three-year-old Oscar received a gift that would one day change his life. The boy's father gave Oscar and his older brother, Joel, each a pair of boxing gloves. In fact, Joel Sr. had bought himself a pair of gloves, too. He wanted to teach his young sons the sport he loved.

The elder Joel had come to the United States from his birthplace in Mexico at the age of 16. He soon started boxing professionally as a way to make some money. Joel knew something about the sport from his father, Vicente, who had also been a boxer. As Joel struggled to make ends meet, thoughts of making it big in the ring could not have been far from his mind. Even in the 1950s and 1960s, the best boxers made much more than the average working man.

It wasn't long before Joel found himself with a record of 9-3-1. While some fighters would have been happy with 9 wins in 14 fights, he knew he was not good enough to make a successful career of fighting in the ring. He

---

Oscar looks on as a young boy learns boxing skills at a youth center in Los Angeles. Oscar survived growing up in a tough neighborhood after his father taught him to box to defend himself.

was just an average fighter at best who needed to get a more typical job. He began what became a long career in the heating and air-conditioning business.

Joel married a young woman, Cecilia, and soon the couple had two sons, Joel Jr. and Oscar, born on February 2, 1973. The boys were born just one year apart from each other. Ceci, the couple's only daughter, would round out the family nine years later. The children grew up in a modest neighborhood of single-family homes, but just blocks from another world of crime, drugs, and gangs.

As Joel boxed on his knees with his two young sons, he was teaching them more than a sport. He was teaching them how to survive in a tough neighborhood. He was giving them something better to do with their time than get involved with gangs.

Yet, even Joel could not have known what the lessons would lead to for his youngest son. At the time, boxing was just a way to keep Oscar out of harm's way, since Joel worried that his younger son was too soft. Oscar seemed to cry more than he talked. He ran from fights, often seeking comfort from his mother. Older brother Joel recalls that his younger brother just was not a fighter. "Oscar hated physical confrontations," he says. Oscar remembers fights this way: "I was a little kid who used to fight a lot in the street—and get beat up, so my father took me to a gym."

Oscar started going to a gym when he was just six years old. To his father's delight, the boy not only liked boxing, he showed a natural talent for it. It was at the Eastside Boxing Club that Oscar met trainer Joe Minjarez. The trainer remembers a scrawny kid, who showed

Mexican immigrants, like this farm worker, maintain strong ties to their heritage. Seeking a better life, Oscar's father came to the United States as a teenager. Oscar is proud of his Mexican roots and his large extended family.

up everyday on his skateboard. Oscar was left-handed, awkwardly leading with his right, trying to land hard punches with the left.

"There was a little kid who was beating him [Oscar] up for about two months," the trainer remembers. "I turned Oscar around to right-handed and within a few days, the kid wouldn't spar with Oscar anymore."

Soon after entering the gym, Oscar had his first official fight. Though there are no official records of the match, Oscar remembers it well. He borrowed everything he wore into the ring the first time. His gloves were too large, and his uncle lent him his shoes, which were five sizes too big. But he knocked his opponent down with his first few punches. "I looked like a clown, with the fronts [of my shoes] all curling up," the young boxer remembers. "But I stopped a kid in the first round. That's when my father said, 'He's gonna be a big champion!'"

By the age of 10, Oscar was going to the Resurrection Boys Club Gym in East Los Angeles, a former church that had been transformed into a gym. Posters in both English and Spanish lined the walls with images of boxers who had come before him. The pictures made a definite impression on the youngster with the Mexican roots.

Eager to learn and to show what he could do, Oscar developed a reputation as a tough fighter inside the ring despite his slender build. His shyness outside of the ring often lulled opponents into thinking his fierce reputation could not be accurate. They quickly changed their minds, however, after sparring with him for a few rounds.

It was his father who taught Oscar not to take it easy in sparring. Joel was afraid his son would develop bad habits in the ring if he took the practice too lightly. Because of his aggressive style, Oscar had trouble finding sparring partners as time passed. Manuel Torres, the director of boxing at the gym, was often heard telling the eager young fighter to take a break because of his intense style.

Training did not end in the gym, however. At home Joel Sr.'s method of discipline included a heavy dose of boxing lessons. This aggressive

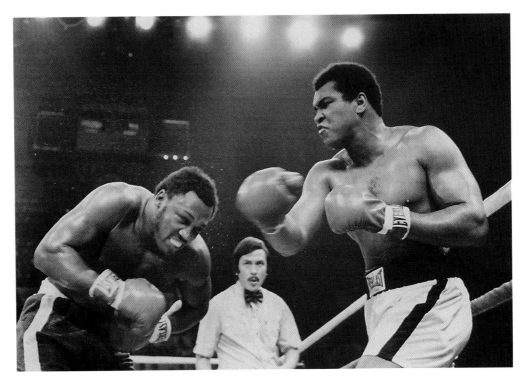

Joe Frazier (left) battles Muhammad Ali in a match in the 1970s. These are two of many boxing legends whose images lined the walls of the gym where Oscar trained as a young boy.

style put him on the road to a great early career in the fight game. Yet, the almost relentless hours of training nearly caused Oscar to leave behind the sport he was perfecting.

One day when he was just 10 years old, Oscar skipped the gym to play with the other kids. He saw them day after day skateboarding after school and wanted to join in. "I was just tired of it," he recalls. "I wanted to be with friends, just hang out, be like a regular, normal kid."

That reason was not good enough for the disciplinarian in Joel Sr., who feared what hanging out could lead to for his son. He ordered Oscar back to the gym the next day. The boy dutifully obeyed and returned to training. But this time his heart simply was not in fighting. Less than a year later Oscar quit boxing, and not just for a day. It seems that Joel Sr. finally realized his son had to make his own decisions.

Of course, boxing was not the only thing keeping Oscar off the streets. He and his brother remained close as they grew up. Oscar's relationship with his brother, and the rest of his family, has been credited with keeping both De La Hoya brothers out of trouble.

The boys also enjoyed the closeness of an extended family, which gathered regularly at a neighborhood restaurant to share meals and talk about their lives. Oscar's grandfather had 16 children from two marriages, most of whom lived within a mile or two of one another. With their help and food stamps, there was nearly always enough to eat. "We never ever felt poor," Oscar remembers. "I mean, even though we were. I know there were times it was tough for us to even have food on the table. We used to borrow it from neighbors or somebody. Luckily, one of my aunts lived next door. So they did us a lot of favors. But we never felt poor. We always felt like we had everything." The De La Hoya family considered these meetings a safety net against the elements of crime that dwelled nearby.

But the hard times did not go completely unnoticed by Oscar. One day his mother sent him to buy groceries with food stamps at a store just six doors from their home. Despite his tears, she insisted he go. When he was ready to pay for the groceries, five or six other people had come into the store. Embarrassed, the boy crouched in the back of the store, waiting for the others to leave. Forty-five minutes passed before he went up to the cashier.

"The lady found me crying, with red eyes,"

Oscar later recalled. When she asked him why he had waited so long to pay, he admitted he was ashamed. "Because I have these little food stamps."

Although the family managed to survive, Oscar had to work his way through high school. Despite the distraction of holding down a job and studying, he was a good student and began considering a career in architecture. He dreamed of majoring in the subject at the University of California at Los Angeles.

During his teen years, Oscar grew especially close to his mother. She was the one both boys turned to for comfort. "You couldn't talk to my dad," he says. "You couldn't go up to my dad and say, 'I love you, Dad,' or, 'Dad, I got good grades in school.' Not that he didn't care, but too macho . . . My mom, she was the one to talk to."

Oscar had probably talked with his mother about boxing when he was 11, because six months after quitting he was back in the ring. It was not that he had gained more machismo or lost interest in his friends. It was not even anything his father said or did. It was much simpler than that. "I missed it," he admits.

A Promise Kept

O nce back in the ring, it was not long before Oscar began earning respect. By the time he was in his early teens, Oscar was becoming well-known in the area around his hometown. Success in local and regional Junior Olympic tournaments was coming fairly easily to him. He gained national attention for the first time when he followed this circuit of tournaments all the way to the top and became the champion in his weight class.

The teenager was rapidly becoming a prospect for the 1992 U.S. Olympic boxing team after his performance in the national tournaments. Some experts even began to suggest he had the talent to be a successful professional boxer someday.

Before that could happen, however, Oscar got his first taste of the famed Golden Gloves tournament in 1987. Numerous boxing greats have competed in this tournament and have established their talents. "Sugar" Ray Leonard and Evander Holyfield are just two of boxing's world champions who first made their mark in this prestigious competition.

His name emblazoned on his trunks, young Oscar shows off his fighting stance. Becoming a national contender in his teens, Oscar established his talents as an amateur boxer and kept a promise to his mother by defeating his challengers and winning a gold medal in the 1992 Olympics.

Oscar became a national contender with one amazing performance in the tournament. He was up against Manuel Nava, who at the time was considered one of the best amateurs in the country. Joe Minjarez, Oscar's trainer at the Eastside Boxing Club, was still training Oscar, and he recalls the fight: "[Oscar] just cleaned him out," he says. "Knocked him down three times. Stopped him. Wow. It was a clean knockout. He'd stopped a lot of kids, but not like he knocked this guy out. He hit him with a left hook and he was *out*."

In the same tournament Oscar fought an older opponent from the U.S. navy. Oscar showed he had the heart of a warrior even against a man who was nine years older. Roberto Alcazar, who then worked with Joel Sr., was a volunteer in Oscar's corner that day. "He was fighting with this twenty-four-year-old man," Alcazar remembers. "So when the fight starts, Oscar got hit on the face. And in the twenty-seven years I've been involved in boxing, I've never seen anything like the expression he had after getting hit. I've never seen that from nobody. It was like a sign from an assassin."

The reaction was also a bit hard to believe. "He really scared me," Alcazar admits. "And in the second round, he knocked the guy out flat. The guy was out. For five minutes he was laying down in the ring. Right from the beginning, I knew [Oscar] was special. That night, everybody knew."

The next year, Oscar found even greater success. Following the same road, he started at the local level and proceeded to national competition. Only this time he was pursuing the Golden Gloves national championship.

He won the featherweight (126-pound) title.

Despite his growing success, Oscar was still a kid. He still had parents to obey and a father who was a strict disciplinarian. One night he was just half a block from his house with his cousins and friends when his nine o'clock curfew hit. He heard his mother call but ignored her. He did not budge when his father called moments later. A few minutes passed, and Oscar thought he had made his point. After all, he thought, he was 16 and could miss curfew once. His father suddenly charged out of the house wearing little more than a robe, screaming at him. "I was never more embarrassed in my life," Oscar says. "Which was the reason why he did it."

The next day the teen fighter pummeled his sparring partner. "Man, it's like inside the ring is where I used to unleash all my frustration," he recalls. "If I was mad at my father that day or anything, I used to go crazy. I used to be

Honored onstage at a Las Vegas television special, Oscar (far right) shares the spotlight with boxing legends (from left) Tommy Hearns, Marvin Hagler, Muhammad Ali, and "Sugar" Ray Leonard. Like Oscar, many boxers got their start as amateurs in Golden Glove tournaments.

crazy inside the ring. Back then, it used to be all anger."

Luckily, Oscar continued to channel that anger into boxing with spectacular results. In 1990 he was off to the Goodwill Games in Seattle, Washington. At age 17, he was the youngest of the 24 U.S. boxers in the competition. He fought fighters from all over the world, including those from the Soviet Union, Cuba, Germany, and Poland.

Despite stepping to a new level of competition, Oscar's amazing success continued. He beat Lee Sang-hun of South Korea in the quarterfinals. The referee stopped the fight in the third round because Sang-hun was so battered. In the semifinals De La Hoya defeated Airat Khamatov of the Soviet Union. Oscar took the gold medal in the finals, beating a fellow U.S. boxer, Ivan Robinson.

Even while Oscar was enjoying his greatest success, his family was hiding a terrible secret from him. His parents kept silent about his mother's diagnosis of cancer so that he could focus on the Goodwill Games. After his gold medal win, Joel Sr. and Cecilia broke the devastating news.

Cecilia had guided her children through a difficult youth. She constantly stressed the importance of education and watched as Oscar did well at Garfield High School in Los Angeles. On at least one occasion Oscar had called her his best friend.

During her battle with cancer, she refused treatments on days Oscar was to fight. She even traveled to Seattle to see him fight in the Goodwill Games. Unfortunately, two months after her son's greatest triumph, Cecilia died at the age of 39. Before she died she made Oscar promise to win the Olympic gold medal for her.

Soon after his mother's funeral, Oscar returned to training. Determined to fulfill his promise to his beloved mother, he began working more furiously than ever. He got up early to run at dawn, often circling the cemetery in which his mother was buried. He also started making little changes to his training style, such as not resting between rounds.

Oscar's string of successes continued in 1991. He defeated Patrice Brooks at the U.S. Olympic Festival in Los Angeles for the lightweight (132-pound) title. He had not lost a fight in nearly five years, and he had never lost to a foreign boxer. At the Olympic Festival he knelt in his corner and blew a kiss heavenward to his mother after each fight.

That same year Oscar graduated from high school. He had developed an obvious talent for art, often sketching coaches and teammates. He knew, however, that he had to put that talent on hold for his other love, boxing. The Olympics were just around the corner, and he had a promise to keep.

At this point, Oscar was certainly attracting notice. He received a lot of coverage in the media, and professional boxing managers and promoters began sizing him up for his potential as a professional. Pat Nappi, the U.S. Olympic boxing coach for the 1976, 1980, and 1984 games, was asked his opinion of the young fighter. "This kid has all the tools," Nappi said. "Right now, based on what I've seen, he has the gold medal."

Oscar was also gaining respect in his own neighborhood. One night while walking to a girlfriend's house, five guys with guns jumped out of a pickup truck. They stole Oscar's camera and his wallet with $150 and his driver's license. Yet, within hours the wallet had been returned to his home with his money still inside. The thugs realized who they had mugged, and even they did not want to harass the local sports hero.

In November 1991, Oscar was off to Sydney, Australia, for the world championships. As usual he breezed through the early fights to make it to the finals. This time, however, the outcome would be different. He faced Germany's Marco Rudolph, a fighter with much more experience in international bouts than himself. Rudolph had also been a world champion. His in-close style stifled Oscar's jabs, and Oscar suffered a 17-13 loss.

Oscar took the loss as a wake-up call, commenting that it was the best thing that could have happened to him. He admitted that Rudolph's "awkward" style threw him off. "I've never seen anything like it," Oscar said. He also said that he had been in a rut and had become bored. He promised to work harder than ever.

Oscar kept his promise. He put in even more hours at the gym and began running even farther. The Olympic trials were just a few months away, and he had to be at his best.

The hard work paid off. In the Olympic trials Oscar's boxing talent, and his long, accurate left jab made him the clear lightweight choice for the U.S. team. He was headed for Barcelona, Spain, to compete in the 1992 Olympic Games.

Just being in the host city was an experience like no other. As Spain's second largest city, Barcelona is considered the country's cultural center. Oscar appreciated its sheer

beauty, marveling at the winding streets, rolling hills, and amazing architecture. He was also delighted to have the chance to connect with his roots, speaking his second language, Spanish, and enjoying the local culture.

The young boxer also enjoyed the atmosphere of the Olympic Village, the area where most of the Olympians lived during the games. He had the opportunity to meet other boxers, as well as other athletes, from nations all over the world. It came as a pleasant surprise for him to hear so many other Olympians speak either English or Spanish.

Of course, Oscar spent most of his days training and honing his skills. The basic, heavy training for the Olympics had already been done prior to arriving in Barcelona. At this point it was up to the athletes to strike a

Sydney, Australia, was the scene of one of Oscar's few defeats as an amateur. When he lost in the finals of the world championships there in 1991, he became more determined than ever to work harder and win in the upcoming Olympics.

balance between staying fit as well as focused and fresh for competition.

As the boxing competition was about to begin, the media was reporting that U.S. fighters were worried about a new computerized scoring system that would be used for the first time in actual competition at Barcelona.

The new scoring system had been established because of a controversy at the previous Olympic Games in Seoul, South Korea. During the boxing competitions in Seoul, millions had watched as American fighter Roy Jones Jr. dominated the gold-medal bout. Then, spectators were shocked when South Korean boxer Park Si-hun was declared the winner.

At the time, the Olympic boxing matches were scored the same way that professional boxing matches are scored. Judges simply watched each round and subjectively scored each one. Though boxing results can often be debated, most everyone agreed that in the Seoul match Jones had defeated Park Si-hun. Headlines screamed that Jones had been robbed of the gold medal. Charges swirled that the judges had been bribed. Others claimed anti-American sentiment was to blame. Whatever the case may have been, a new scoring system was clearly needed.

So, judging boxing matches—at least those in Olympic competition—entered the computer age. Under the new system, judges pressed a button each time they felt a fighter landed a punch. Three of the five judges had to hit the button for the same fighter within one second of one another for a blow to count.

The system, however, was far from perfect. On the second night of the boxing competition, Oscar realized just how flawed the new and supposedly more accurate scoring could be. He saw his teammate, 106-pound light flyweight Eric Griffin, get robbed. Fighters in the light weight divisions typically throw a lot of punches. However, in Griffin's match, for all three rounds combined only 11 total punches were counted—5 for Griffin and 6 for Rafael Lozano of Spain.

When it was Oscar's turn to fight, he had to put the controversy out of his mind. Making the task even more difficult was the knowledge that he and Griffin had been considered the United States' best hopes for a gold medal in boxing. Now, it was up to him.

His quarterfinal opponent was Moses Odion of Nigeria, who was a tall fighter with a longer reach than Oscar's. In the first of the three rounds, Oscar jabbed Odion repeatedly but only won the round by a score of 1-0. Olympic coach Joe Byrd urged Oscar to pick up his pace. Spurred on by the coach, Oscar dominated the next two rounds and won the fight 16-4.

Just two nights later, Oscar went up against Tontcho Tontchev from Bulgaria. It would be a difficult match for Oscar. Tontchev had beaten a Cuban in his first bout. Boxers from Cuba are considered to be among the toughest amateur fighters in the world. Living in a Communist country, they are not free to turn pro and often spend their entire careers as overqualified amateurs.

Still, Oscar passed the test with flying colors, proving to be too quick for his opponent. He again dominated with jabs and crushing upper-cuts. The same problems occurred with the scoring system, however, giving Oscar a narrow victory in the first round. Once again, he stepped up his pace and won comfortably, 16-7.

In the 1992 Olympic semifinals, Oscar (left) swings at Hong Sung-Sik of South Korea. Thrown off at first by his opponent's rowdy style, Oscar rallied and beat Hong by one point, moving on to the finals.

As expected, Oscar's semifinal opponent was his toughest match. South Korean Hong Sung-Sik had knocked out a previous opponent with a body blow that demonstrated great strength. To make matters worse, Oscar felt sluggish. He had fought a lot of matches in a short period of time.

Oscar was cautious early on while the tall, slender Hong Sung-Sik pounced. His brawling style threw Oscar off guard. The South Korean fighter was warned and penalized three points in the second round for getting Oscar in a headlock and for head-butting. Oscar retaliated in the third and received the same penalty. But he held on to win the fight by the slimmest of margins, 11-10. Coach Byrd said of this semifinal fight, "We were just lucky. That could have gone either way."

Finally, the time to fight for the gold medal had arrived. As fate would have it, in the finals Oscar would face Marco Rudolph of Germany—the only international opponent who had ever beaten him. By now Oscar was tired, and he had injured his thumb in the previous bout, but there was no time for excuses.

Joel Sr. was with his son in Barcelona, and he told Oscar it was time to win: "You're taller than he is, and you've got a longer reach," he said. "You've got to take advantage of those things. Keep sticking him and move, move, move."

Oscar stepped out and dominated round one, only to see a score of 1-1. He mixed up punches well in the second round—jabbing and doing damage with uppercuts. He even stunned his opponent but was only given the round by a point, 3-2.

Entering the final round of the gold-medal bout leading by just one point, Oscar could not make any mistakes. A furious exchange between the two fighters, including a left hook to Rudolph's chin, dropped the German. He rose to his feet and took the standing eight count.

When the bell finally rang, Oscar threw up his hands in victory, and Rudolph hugged him, knowing Oscar had won, 7-2. Then, dropping to one knee, Oscar raised a hand heavenward. He had kept his promise to his mother and had won the Olympic gold medal, the only U.S. boxer to win the gold that year.

Jubilant in his victory, Oscar circled the ring proudly waving little U.S. and Mexican

Proudly holding his Olympic gold medal, Oscar receives the cheers of the crowd in Barcelona in 1992. For the young Mexican-American fighter, his win was a double triumph. He kept his promise to his mother to win a gold medal, and he was the only U.S. boxer to come home with the gold.

flags. "I went up [to the Olympics] with the Mexican flag and the American flag," he said. "If I'd had enough arms I would have gone up with all the flags of the world."

The young man who prided himself on being macho admitted that emotion almost got the best of him as the band played "The Star Spangled Banner." Oscar said: "I was afraid I might start to cry but then I figured my mom would say, 'Don't cry, be happy—you won the gold medal.'"

Referring to why he boxes, Oscar later remarked: "I fight first for my mother, then my family, then myself, then for all the people who support me—the Mexican people, all Hispanic people. I fight for the whole world."

4

TURNING PRO

After the Olympics, Oscar wanted to return to school and study architecture. But his father encouraged him to take a $21-million deal from HBO (Home Box Office) for the broadcast rights to his fights. Joel Sr. knew it was a once-in-a-lifetime offer. "I started to realize that I had to think about my future," Oscar says. "I had to think about if [my mother] were here, how she would want my life to progress. I had to think about all the people who helped me, so I could pay them back."

Still, Oscar realized that fame could be fleeting. His popularity as the only U.S. boxer to bring home the gold would not last forever. Oscar took the HBO deal, which would air his fights once he began challenging other boxers for their titles. With the decision to turn professional, Oscar would have to start at the bottom again.

Even so, he would still be under the media spotlight. With his Olympic gold medal came name recognition, which in turn brought attention and even some criticism.

It was assumed Oscar would sign with boxing promoter Shelley Finkel when he became a pro fighter. After all, Finkel

---

A gigantic banner attached to the side of a building broadcasts one of Oscar's fights as a professional. With his amazing fight record as an amateur and his soaring popularity, Oscar decided he could not turn down an HBO offer to turn pro and continue his boxing career.

had done many favors for Oscar as an amateur, including flying him to other cities to spar with better partners. Once he even flew Oscar and his family to a title bout they wanted to see.

Then, the promoting team of Bob Mittelman and Steve Nelson entered the picture in a big way, offering to promote Oscar's fights. They produced a contract that called for Oscar to receive $500,000 in cash, a new car and van, and another $500,000 for a down payment on a four-bedroom home in Montebello, a luxurious Los Angeles neighborhood. The deal was too good to pass up, and Oscar accepted.

After signing the contract, Oscar got his first taste of the price to be paid for being in the celebrity spotlight. Many sharply criticized him for not signing a deal with Finkel. Not only was it seen as disloyal, it also seemed as though Oscar had taken the money instead of the expertise Finkel could have offered him.

With Finkel, he would have been under the guidance of the highly respected trainer Dino Duva, who has trained welterweight champion Pernell "Sweet Pee" Whitaker as well as cruiser and heavyweight champion Evander Holyfield. Oscar also would have had the benefit of one of the world's best trainers in George Benton.

Having compiled an amazing record of 223 wins and just 5 losses as an amateur, Oscar had not faced much public scrutiny. Still, his fast pace early on in his new career helped him put the criticism behind him. In his very first professional fight, on November 23, 1992, he scored a first-round knockout versus Lamar Williams.

Boxing analyst Jimmy Lennon Jr., who announced the fight, gave Oscar the nickname "Golden Boy" after this fight. For his first pro fight, Oscar earned $150,000—probably more

than his father had made in all of his professional fights combined. A few weeks later, on December 12, he knocked out Clifford "Bobo" Hicks in one round. But Oscar had to go two rounds to earn a technical knockout (TKO)—meaning a fighter cannot continue—against Paris Alexander on January 3, 1993.

It was a great start to Oscar's professional career, but critics questioned whether he could keep up the intense pace. Some said that being pushed by his handlers, promoters, trainers, and advisers was about to catch up to him. It

In match after match, Oscar scored in the ring and with his growing following of enthusiastic fans. Here a crowd cheers him at a bout in El Paso, Texas.

was not actually the number of fights the critics were questioning. Many young fighters begin their careers at a fast pace. Generally, however, they face competition that is just as inexperienced or not very good.

Oscar, with only four professional rounds under his belt, was up against a very solid opponent when he met Curtis Strong in February 1993. Strong had 22 professional fights under his belt and experience boxing in 10-round "main events." This meant he was good enough to be in the headliner of a particular card of fights. For example, a big fight such as a heavyweight title bout may be *the* fight people have paid to see on a particular night. But several fights—called the undercard—take place leading up to the main fight. All of the fights as a group, including the main one, are referred to as the card.

Doubts about Oscar's ability to handle the better competition were laid to rest rather quickly. He dominated the first round, even knocking Strong to the canvas. The fight was called to a halt in the fourth round—Oscar won. A little more than a month later, on March 13, Oscar took another step up in competition. He earned a technical knockout against 24-2-2 veteran fighter Jeremy Mayweather, again stopping his opponent in four rounds.

Oscar finally went the distance in his sixth professional fight. He entered the ring against Mike Grable, who was also a young fighter with potential. Grable had a professional record of 13-1-2 and had recorded more than 100 wins as an amateur. He had also displayed knockout ability of his own—he had knocked out half of his pro opponents.

Again, Oscar rose to the challenge. He dropped Grable several times, although the fight went all eight rounds. Oscar won in an easy decision on all the judges' scorecards.

While Oscar did not deliver a knockout, he did receive one of the finest compliments a young fighter can get. USA Cable Network boxing analyst Sean O'Grady called him "the future of boxing."

Oscar planned to live up to O'Grady's words by setting an astonishing goal: to win championship belts in the junior lightweight, lightweight, junior welterweight, welterweight, junior middleweight, and middleweight divisions. The accomplishment would make him the first Hispanic to win titles in six different weight classes.

Oscar won the first on March 5, 1994. He took a relatively minor belt, the World Boxing Organization (WBO)'s lightweight crown from 130-pound king Jimmi Bredahl. Oscar won via a technical knockout in the 10th round.

A few months later, Oscar fought Jorge Paez for the WBO junior lightweight title, scoring a second-round knockout. Three fights later, Oscar faced one of his most severe tests in the ring. Former world champion John John Molina caused Oscar some problems on February 18, 1995, but the Golden Boy won in a unanimous decision.

Finally, in his 18th pro fight Oscar fought for a respected title. He met Rafael Ruelas in Las Vegas for the International Boxing Federation's lightweight crown. The fight, on May 6, 1995, saw Oscar earn a victory by a technical knockout. Four fights later Oscar defeated Chávez for the WBC's super lightweight title. Then, he overcame Pernell Whitaker on April 12, 1997, in Las Vegas for the WBC welterweight crown.

Oscar was taking on all challengers and

Nineteen ninety-seven was a banner year for Oscar—he defeated all comers and won the welterweight title. Here, he holds up the welterweight belt he earned defeating Pernell Whitaker in 12 grueling rounds.

coming out on top—a rare occurrence in boxing during the 1990s. Most premiere fighters took relatively easy fights to keep their records unblemished. "Boxing is in a sad state," boxing legend "Sugar" Ray Leonard said. "The only young man out there doing a thing is Oscar De La Hoya. Oscar De La Hoya is the only one I think making a difference in boxing."

Oscar was certainly busy making a difference in 1997. After fighting Whitaker (and stopping challenger David Kamau in round two of their June 1997 title fight in San Antonio, Texas), he met another well-respected fighter—and one of the flashiest. In September of that year, several of Oscar's punches wobbled former world champion Hector "Macho" Camacho. Although Camacho managed to survive 12 rounds, Oscar retained his WBC welterweight title. He finished out the year defeating Wilfredo Rivera, a eighth-round TKO victim. By the fight's end, Rivera could attest to the fact that Oscar had significant power in his right hand.

Prior to his first fight of that busy 1997—a 12-round victory by decision on January 18 over Miguel Angel Gonzalez in Las Vegas— Oscar said, "I want to be considered as one of the great legends who fought the best and beat the best." Twelve months later he had left little doubt that he meant every word.

After beating Whitaker, the sky seemed to be the limit. Some even suggested Oscar would be as big an attraction and as popular as Mike Tyson. Unlike many fighters who stay on well past their prime, however, Oscar might actually leave boxing before he reaches his peak. "I want to fight the best fighters in the world and retire at a young age," he has said. "When I do retire, I won't come back."

IN AND OUT
OF THE RING

While Oscar has had tremendous success as a boxer, life is more than being inside the ring. He seems to have a firm grasp on what he wants from his career. As many young people find out, however, achieving one's goals is not always easy.

Some suggest that Oscar is on a quest for the perfect fight. Apparently, he does not disagree. "Maybe in three years or so, I'll give a perfect performance," he said after his 27th straight victory, when he defeated Wilfredo Rivera on December 6, 1997, in Atlantic City. Then he added: "And maybe not. Maybe I'll retire by then."

Oscar was alluding to the fact that he has every intention of retiring at a young age. But that goal will require financial responsibility, something he struggled with early in his career. In fact, the way he handled money even caused a brief rift in Oscar's relationship with his father.

The young fighter may have shown family loyalty after his first fight, but his father felt he didn't show much responsibility about money. The first thing Oscar did after

Welterweight champion Oscar (left) with his trainer Roberto Alcazar (right) is surrounded by adoring fans as he signs autographs. Problems with trainers such as Alcazar, as well as his lifestyle outside the ring, have made Oscar realize that success and celebrity are sometimes difficult to handle.

receiving his pay was to buy several brand-new skateboards. Of course, he also bought his family a four-bedroom house.

The fall out that ensued with Joel Sr. over money was soon repaired. Mike Hernandez, known for helping young Latinos manage money, was brought in to help Oscar, who seemed to get the message. "I'm not gonna be another statistic in boxing," Oscar said. "They're not going to say, 'He's just another fighter like any of the others: He made money, he lost it, and didn't make [anything] of himself.'" In fact, Oscar still keeps a food stamp in his wallet to remember the hard times he overcame.

Oscar is still young, however, and his drive to deliver the perfect fight may be doing more harm than good. Several lead trainers have been in his corner, and some suggest that his ambition to be perfect is to blame. Hall of Fame trainer Emmanuel Steward was hired then fired after just a few fights. Others have also made quick exits.

Roberto Alcazar, Oscar's first trainer, was relatively inexperienced at the time, but he was a friend of Joel Sr.'s. Nevertheless, Alcazar was soon pushed aside for the more experienced Carlos Ortiz, a boxing Hall of Famer light-weight fighter in the late 1950s. Oscar was not very receptive to Ortiz's extremely intense training and dismissed him too.

Next, Oscar hired Jesus Rivero, who had guided Miguel Canto to the lightweight title. At first Rivero seemed to be a perfect fit for Oscar. He was even in Oscar's corner for his first bout with Chávez. But when the trainer began hogging too much of the spotlight, he was also sent on his way.

Emmanuel Steward returned and took over

one more time. He was expected to restore Oscar's aggressive style after Rivero had stressed defense. The result was two dominating victories in 1997 against Kamau and Camacho. But Steward too was dismissed again, and Alcazar was reinstated as trainer. "It's like golf," Oscar explained. "If a teacher is not helping you, you get another one until your game is right or perfect. You have to keep improving."

Oscar is also serious about other aspects of his life. He has not forgotten about his desire to continue his education. "I'd like to go back to school," he says. "I've encouraged kids to pursue an education because it's very important to me. I've developed my skills as a boxer. After that I've got to develop my mind."

He is certainly interested in helping other young Latinos do the same. Oscar offers scholarships to assist youngsters from his community to pursue their education. He founded the renovation of an old gym in East Los Angeles, which is now called the Oscar De La Hoya Boxing Youth Center. "I go back to schools to speak to kids about their futures," he says. "Just because they are Hispanic, they shouldn't feel left out or below someone else— we should all feel equal. I grew up without having anything in my life."

In recent years Oscar has also had to contend with new experiences in and out of the ring. He has become one of the most well-known celebrities in the country. His good-guy image makes him extremely likeable to the public and therefore extremely marketable. By 1997, Oscar was the third-highest-paid athlete in the world, having made $38 million in wins and endorsements. Only basketball star Michael Jordan ($78.3 million) and heavyweight champion Evander

Holyfield ($54.3 million) made more then the young boxer that year.

At the age of 24, Oscar was the most marketable fighter in the history of boxing. The endorsement offers continued to pour in. He served as the national spokesman for Anheuser-Busch's "Know When to Say When" campaign promoting responsible drinking. He was part of the campaign to drink milk and has been seen in trendy men's magazines modeling the latest fashions. One magazine reported that for every endorsement Oscar accepts, he turns down about 10.

Oscar's celebrity status has also opened his personal life to public scrutiny. In December 1999 he was accused of rape. While no details were released, the charge was substantial enough to be investigated. His attorney, Robert Chapman, asserted that the charges were false. "Unfortunately, celebrities are often the subject of these sort of false stories," Chapman said. Fans of the fighter certainly hope that these claims are not true.

Oscar is also dealing with the consequences of romancing a long string of girlfriends. On February 18, 1998, his son, Jacob, was born. Although he welcomed fatherhood, the revelation that he had a son on the way cost him a relationship with a woman to whom he was engaged to be married. Then, in December 1999, it was reported that the boxer was engaged to Shanna Moakler, an actress on the USA Network's *Pacific Blue* series. Their daughter, Atiana Cecilia De La Hoya, was born in March of that year.

As if his relationships were not enough to keep Oscar occupied, he is apparently set to try his hand at a new profession—music.

HILLARY'S FOES ★ TEEN FLICKS ★ DINOSAUR EGGS

Newsweek

www.newsweek.c   July 12, 1999 : $3.50

Latin

How Young Hispanics Are Changing America

U.S.A.

Author Junot Díaz, singer Shakira, boxer Oscar De La Hoya

Oscar (forefront) appears on the cover of Newsweek *magazine. His immense popularity has thrust him into the limelight and brought distractions that some feel have affected his boxing career.*

The website of the entertainment network *E!* reports that the record label EMI Latin plans to release Oscar's debut music album.

One can only wonder if Oscar's lifestyle is becoming a distraction in the ring. Oscar suffered his first loss as a professional on September 18, 1999, when he was defeated in Las Vegas by Felix Trinidad, the IBF champion from Puerto Rico.

Trinidad came into the fight with 30 knockouts compared to Oscar's 25. The sellout crowd of 11,610 expected fireworks from the opening bell. What they got instead was Oscar's

Oscar appears at a benefit for the Oscar De La Hoya Foundation with his girlfriend Shanna Moakler. Founded by Oscar, the foundation supports athletic and educational opportunities to children in East Los Angeles.

picture-perfect match for several rounds and an exhibition of tenacity by Trinidad.

As the match opened, Oscar seemed to have the upper hand. Trinidad was clearly outboxed through the early rounds, but he would not give up. Fighting off Oscar, Trinidad came on in the late rounds, controlling the fight with some crashing rights to the head. Although Oscar never appeared ready to go down, he felt the power of the punches and chose to peddle away from his opponent's bombardment. Trinidad earned the title by fighting for it in the final three rounds. Trinidad's victory took the WBC welterweight title from Oscar, keeping the Puerto Rican boxer unbeaten in 36 fights.

Judge Glen Hamada of Tacoma, Washington, scored the fight 114-114. Judge Jerry Roth of Las Vegas saw it 115-113 in favor of Trinidad, and Judge Bob Logiste of Belgium had it 115-114 for Trinidad. Trinidad won all of the last three rounds and the fight on two of the scorecards.

Following his victory, Trinidad declared that "Oscar deserves a rematch." Then he asked Oscar, "Am I worth $10.5 million?" The remark reflected Trinidad's annoyance at Oscar's comment before the fight that Trinidad did not deserve $10 million for the bout. Trinidad actually got $8.5 million, while Oscar was guaranteed $15 million.

"Hopefully, we can do it again," the 26-year-old Oscar said. "I wanted to demonstrate my boxing skills, but I guess it didn't work. To my fans, I am very sorry. I love you guys, I will be back." Clearly disappointed, the young boxer added, "Obviously, in my heart I thought I won the fight. Next time, I will be a brawler." He also said he would take a vacation to clear his head.

Oscar responded to criticism from his loss the best way he knew how—in the ring. He fought Darrell Coley in New York City on February 26, 2000, and returned to his aggressive style. Pressing Coley throughout the fight, Oscar wobbled him in the fourth round with several pounding body blows. He continued the onslaught for three more rounds. Finally, his right eye swollen shut from left hooks, Coley took one last left to the stomach and went to his knees.

Coley was counted out as the seventh round ended. "I felt good at 147 [pounds]," Oscar said after the fight. "My plan is to fight four times this year and get four knockouts. Coley was the first."

Instead of the rematch with Trinidad, which was what Oscar wanted, Shane Mosley would be his next opponent. Oscar seemed unconcerned, however. "It doesn't matter which is first, I think I will fight the two of them this year in whatever order," he said prior to signing a deal to fight Mosley. "The next fight will be sometime in June. If it's Shane Mosley or Trinidad, it's all the same for me. I will be in good shape, and they will have to adjust to me. It's all about me having the confidence to bang for 12 rounds if I have to. I am going to stick to my guns."

Oscar insisted his first professional loss was actually a good thing. "Trinidad was a blessing in disguise," he said. "Boxing him for 12 rounds obviously did not work and it changed my whole mentality and the way I approach boxing. . . . I was feeling I was unstoppable and couldn't lose, and this loss with Trinidad was the best thing that can happen to me. Thank you Trinidad, it is bringing out the best in me."

Oscar's match with Mosley took on more importance for him even before the fight began. Oscar was awarded the WBC welterweight title he lost to Trinidad, who had moved up to a higher weight class. The WBC gave Oscar the title based on his victory against Coley. "On June 17, [2000], this belt goes along with the title," a confident Oscar said of his bout with Mosley, which had suddenly become a title defense.

In the meantime, Oscar had decided to take on even more outside-the-ring business. Just four days after the Mosley fight, Oscar planned to play a key role in a meeting to discuss a boxers' union. An idea first introduced by the great Jack Dempsey in a 1937 letter to the *New York Times*, it has been beaten down time after time by controlling promoters and managers.

Oscar hopes this time things will turn out differently. Unlike fighters before him who failed, he has some interesting allies in his corner. Senator John Micatin, author of the Muhammad Ali Boxing Protection Bill, backs the effort. So too do authors Norman Mailer and Budd Schulberg as well as former New York City mayor and former fighter David Dinkins. Other boxers are also in Oscar's corner, including former champions Ali and George Foreman and current champions Lennox Lewis, Roy Jones Jr., Bernard Hopkins, Prince Naseem Hamed, and Fernando Vargas.

Other unions are also adding to the support for a boxers' union. The United Auto Workers, the railroad unions, the Screen Actors' Guild, Gene Upshaw and the NFL Players' Association, and all the other major-league players' associations are behind the effort.

Unlike previous failed efforts, the groundwork has been painstakingly laid by a slowtalking former Vietnam marine and railroad cop from Minnesota named Paul Johnson. A one-time middleweight and a one-time walk-on defensive back at the University of Minnesota, Johnson has virtually made a boxers' union his life's work.

Johnson planned to meet with Oscar the week after the fight and present the union and pension plans that he has been working on since 1984. Johnson said Oscar has the resolve to rally boxing, the only major sport without a union, pension, or health insurance

Oscar is honored by GQ magazine as Man of the Year in 1999 for Individual Sports Athlete. Despite recent loses in the ring, Oscar is determined to succeed, whether in the ring or outside his chosen profession.

plan. "This is something he really wants to do," Johnson said. Despite his enthusiasm, however, Oscar's involvement, along with his other distractions, may be too much for him.

The fight with Mosley turned out to be Oscar's second loss in three bouts. The match was very close as the two boxers battled it out in the last round. Mosley landed 45 of 88 punches to 18 of 72 for Oscar in the final three minutes.

Mosley needed that round to win the fight,

and the judges scored the match for him. Judge Lou Filippo gave Mosley 116-112, Pat Russell favored Mosley as well, 115-113, and Marqi Samon scored it 115-113 for Oscar. If Russell had given Oscar the last round, his score would have been 114-114, and Oscar would have kept the title on a draw. Mosley had upset Oscar for the WBC welterweight championship.

"There has to be a rematch,"Oscar said afterward. "Every great fight deserves a rematch. He's a great champion. People got their money's worth. He kept on coming. He was in great condition. He had good power."

It seems Oscar has come to a crossroads in his career. Whether he erases the memory of the recent stretch of two out of three losses and eliminates distraction—or copes better with life outside the ring—only time will tell. That is, time and the strength and determination of Oscar De La Hoya.

CAREER STATS

YEAR	DATE	EVENT	ROUND	WINS
1992	November 23	defeats Lamar Williams	1	ko
	December 12	defeats Clifford Hicks	1	ko
1993	January 3	defeats Paris Alexander	2	tko
	February 6	defeats Curtis Strong	4	tko
	March 13	defeats Jeremy Mayweather	4	ko
	April 6	defeats Mike Grable	8	decision
	May 8	defeats Frank Avelar	4	tko
	June 7	defeats Troy Dorsey	1	tko
	August 14	defeats Renaldo Carter	6	ko
	August 27	defeats Angelo Nunez	4	tko
	October 30	defeats Narcisco Valenzuela	1	ko
1994	March 5	defeats Jimmi Bredahl	10	tko
	May 27	defeats Giorgio Campanella	3	ko
	July 29	defeats Jorge Paez	2	ko
	November 18	defeats Carl Griffith	3	ko
	December 10	defeats John Avila	9	tko
1995	February 18	defeats John John Molina	12	decision
	May 6	defeats Rafael Ruelas (wins IBF lightweight title)	2	tko
	September 9	defeats Genaro Hernandez	6	tko
	December 15	defeats James Leija	2	tko
1996	February 9	defeats Darryl Tyson	2	ko
	June 7	defeats Julio César Chávez (wins WBC super lightweight title)	4	tko
1997	January 18	defeats Miguel Angel Gonzalez	12	decision
	April 12	defeats Pernell Whitaker (wins WBC welterweight title)	12	decision
	June 14	defeats David Kamau	2	ko
	September 13	defeats Hector Camacho	12	decision
	December 6	defeats Wilfredo Rivera	8	tko

1998	June 13	defeats Patrick Charpentier	3	tko
	September 18	defeats Julio César Chávez	8	tko

1999	February 13	defeats Ike Quartey	12	decision
	May 22	defeats Oba Carr	11	tko
	September 18	loses to Felix Trinidad (loses WBC welterweight title)	12	decision

2000	February 26	defeats Darrell Coley	7	ko
	June 17	loses to Shane Mosely	12	decision

Career Totals*:

- 32 Wins
- 2 Losses
- 11 Knockouts
- 15 Technical Knockouts

ko - knockout

tko - technical knockout

decision - win by points

* as of June 17, 2000

CHRONOLOGY

1973	Born February 2 to Cecilia and Joel De La Hoya in Los Angeles.
1979	Begins learning boxing.
1988	Wins the Golden Gloves national championship title in the featherweight (126-pound) division.
1990	Wins a gold medal at the Goodwill Games; mother dies.
1991	Wins the lightweight (132-pound) title at U.S. Olympic Festival; graduates from high school; travels to Sydney, Australia, for world championship competition.
1992	Wins Olympic gold medal in Barcelona, Spain; turns professional; signs a $21-million deal with HBO; wins first pro fight with a knockout over Lamar Williams in one round.
1994	Defeats Jimmi Bredahl in March to earn his first professional title—World Boxing Organization (WBO) Junior Lightweight.
1995	Defeats first noteworthy opponent, John John Molina, in February; wins International Boxing Federation (IBF) lightweight title in May by defeating Rafael Ruelas.
1996	Defeats his idol Julio César Chávez in June.
1997	Wins the World Boxing Council (WBC) welterweight title in April by defeating Pernell Whitaker.
1998	Son, Jacob, born on February 18.
1999	Daughter, Atiana Cecilia, born in March; defeated by Felix Trinidad and loses WBC welterweight title; gets engaged to Shanna Moakler.
2000	Defeats Darrell Coley in February; loses to Shane Mosely in June.

FURTHER READING

Avila, Alex. *Oscar De La Hoya, Boxing's Golden Boy*. Los Angeles: Lowell House, 1998.

Kawakami, Tim. *The Golden Boy: The Fame, Money, and Mystery of Oscar De La Hoya*. Kansas City: Andrews & McMeel, 1999.

Menard, Valerie. *Oscar De La Hoya*. Childs, Md.: Mitchell Lane Publishers, 1999.

Saraceno, Jon. *12 Rounds with Oscar De La Hoya*. Dallas: Beckett Publications, 1998.

Taylor, Robert. *Oscar De La Hoya, Boxing's Boy Wonder*. Florida: Rourke Enterprises, 1993.

Torres, John Albert. *Sports Great Oscar De La Hoya*. Springfield, N.J.: Enslow Publishers, 1998.

PHOTO CREDITS:

Chris Weeks/NEWSMAKERS: 2; Roger Williams/UPI: 6, 14; Steve W. Grayson/ UPI: 9; Icon SMI: 11; Chris Pizzello/AP/Wide World Photos: 16; New Millennium Images: 19, 31, 51; Showtime/Feature Photo Service: 21; Marc Morrison/Zuma Press: 24; Jack Dempsey/AP/Wide World Photos: 27; Bill Sikes/AP/Wide World Photos: 34; Mark Duncan/AP/Wide World Photos: 36; OLUSA: 38; J. R. Hernandez/UPI: 41; Nasser Khan/UPI: 44; Roger Williams/NEWSMAKERS: 46; Jim Ruymen/UPI: 52; Ezio Petersen/UPI: 56.

INDEX

ABOUT THE AUTHOR

ROB QUINN is an assistant editor at Chelsea House Publishers and has experience as a freelance writer for the *Philadelphia Inquirer.* This is his first published book.